Seeds of
Wisdom and
Heavenly
Inspirations

Daily Reflections
from the Spirit World

KIMBERLY KLEIN

Copyrighted Material

Seeds of Wisdom and Heavenly Inspirations

Copyright © 2015 by Kimberly Klein. All Rights Reserved.

No part of this publication may be reproduced, stored in a retrieval system, or transmitted, in any form or by any means—electronic, mechanical, photocopying, recording, or otherwise—without prior written permission from the publisher, except for the inclusion of brief quotations in a review.

For information about this title or to order other books and/or electronic media, contact the publisher:
PMA Press
www.pmapress.com
info@pmapress.com

ISBN: 978-0-9881787-3-1

Printed in the United States of America
Cover and Interior design: 1106 Design

Introduction

THERE ARE NUMEROUS daily quote books out there for you to read—hundreds of them, in fact. Some are philosophical, some are religious, some are humorous, and some are inspirational. What makes this book, *Seeds of Wisdom and Heavenly Inspirations,* different from all those others is that every single quote in this book has been given to us directly from the spirit world, without interference.

What does that mean, *without interference?* It means that there are no religious tones, no interpretations made for you, and no "spin" at all to direct you to believe in a specific religion or system of thought. Every quote is there for you to garner any knowledge, wisdom, insight, or direction that you need at the time you're reading it. You can read and reflect on one quote per day, starting with Day 1 and reading consecutively, or you can just open the book to any page and browse. The quote that hits you the most is likely to be just what you need at the time.

What are these quotes about, and where do they come from? These quotes are about love and life, how to live authentically as yourself, connecting with the Oneness a lot of us are searching for, and the reality of our lives in the body as well as in the spirit. They are taken from Books One and Two of *The Universe Speaks: A Heavenly Dialogue*.

The dialogues in these books are direct communications, recorded at the exact time they occurred, between Talia, my daughter, in the spirit world, and a man we call "G." They began about a month after Talia died, when the small private plane she was in crashed into the side of a volcano in Panama just after her thirteenth birthday.

In *The Universe Speaks: A Heavenly Dialogue,* Talia teaches us that the conversations between the spirit world and those of us in physical bodies are as normal and natural as any conversation between two people on earth. Presenting firsthand, unequivocal accounts of "heaven," she describes what it's like to transition from the physical world to nonphysical realms. And she shows us that death is a gateway into a new realm of life.

Book One of *The Universe Speaks* offers peace to those who fear death, insight into our lives on earth and the world beyond, and understanding to anyone who has been affected by tragedy. Book Two of *The Universe Speaks* takes us deeper into the world of the spirit. Continuing the themes of Book One, this book goes even deeper into the workings of the spirit, and it teaches us the how-tos for living up to our birthright: our ability to be in relationship with our true selves, with the Universe, and with God—the Oneness we all seek.

The quotes in *Seeds of Wisdom and Heavenly Inspirations* are organized into those from Books One and Two of *The Universe Speaks*. The quotes are taken directly from these conversations. A few small formatting alterations have been made, as well as some condensing of quotes, for ease of readability in a stand-alone quotation form. But Talia's words have not been altered; her meaning has been left as given, with no twists or modifications whatsoever to the intent of her words.

Seeds of Wisdom and Heavenly Inspirations is for those of you looking for inspiration or a deeper understanding of life, both in the body and after we shed our physical being. If you are looking for words of wisdom that come directly from the spirit world—rather than from another physical being passing on his or her own thoughts and interpretations—then these quotes will inspire you, expand your thoughts, and bring you joy and understanding of the deepest and most real questions of all: Who are we? What does it mean to live and to die? What is our purpose?

THE UNIVERSE SPEAKS
A Heavenly Dialogue

Kimberly Klein

Book One

Day 1

Always believe yourself.

―――

Book 1

Day 2

Think your own thoughts and not what people tell you to think. If you're thinking someone else's thoughts, how can you be free? It's your birthright to be free. It's a yearning everyone has. So why would someone make a prison for others to live in?

Book 1

Day 3

There are so many truths, so MANY paths, but only one true GOD.

Book 1

Day 4

There's a difference knowing something in your head and KNOWING something in your heart, in your spirit, in your soul, deep down.

Book 1

Day 5

As you think in your heart, so are you.

Book 1

Day 6

The whole universe is on a vibrational level for balance to maintain harmony. That's why it's easy to tell if someone is out of harmony; their very essence is not vibrating in harmony.

Book 1

Day 7

Your thoughts are more real than anything else there [on this plane of existence]. They truly create.

Book 1

Day 8

The nature of reality is living real. BEING true and speaking the truth out of a sincere heart CHANGES things.

Book 1

Day 9

Truth: sometimes it hurts, but it does bring relief, and healing if applied correctly. Don't be harsh or brutal with it.

Book 1

Day 10

The future is not written in stone. Most of it's decided by the decisions of man. To accept or reject are close decisions.

Book 1

Day 11

Forgiveness is the key to freedom. You must forgive everyone, no matter what they did to you or what you think they did to you. A key component is to be AWARE of it. Sometimes you can judge without being aware.

Book 1

Day 12

People can easily convince themselves they're something they are not. They are made in the Creator's image. That inherently gives them the power and ability to create; therefore, they are, in a manner of speaking, the masters of their destiny. If people realized this, they could change the course of their lives into anything they want.

Book 1

Day 13

The kingdom of Heaven is WITHIN you.

Book 1

Day 14

People receive these messages [from the Spirit] all of the time, but most ignore them as a stray thought or their imagination.

Book 1

Day 15

There really are no problems,
only lessons to be learned.

Book 1

Day 16

The truth can bear any and all manner of scrutiny; a lie cannot bear the light at all.

Book 1

Day 17

The answer to every question is within the very question itself.

Book 1

Day 18

We have the same feelings here [in Heaven], just more perfect.

Book 1

Day 19

Of all the misconceptions,
death is the biggest myth of all.

Book 1

Day 20

You must have an intense desire, a passion even, to achieve enlightenment. What many consider enlightenment is merely knowledge. Enlightenment is walking IN the light.

Book 1

Day 21

The whole foundation of everything that means anything is Truth. Nothing is more absolute, no footing firmer. The Truth is the beginning and the end, yet it has no end or beginning—that's the truth.

Book 1

Day 22

Anything you want
is here [in Heaven].

Book 1

Day 23

It just IS, and there's no end to all you can do here. One is NEVER tired, but filled with hope and a sense of Purpose. The expectations burst forth! There is no within or without. There is no sorrow, pain, or suffering—those are like a distant memory. Your life on earth is SO short, no amount of

(continued on next page)

Day 23 *(continued)*

suffering could ever compare to the glory that is to be. The deepest doubts you ever had there, you could compare to a mist, hardly noticeable. Here you are totally, absolutely, and completely fulfilled. No thing missing. Everything that there is, is here to behold—beauty unspeakable. Words just fail.

Book 1

Day 24

You are part of everything.
You are connected with all
things, with all there is.

Book 1

Day 25

It's ALL recorded in the Book of Life. NOTHING compares with THAT book. It contains everything. Some think it's a figure of speech. It is every word ever spoken. Some think it's just a list of names, because that's how they see it described. It is a list of names, of natures, natures of life.

(continued on next page)

(continued) **Day 25**

All the nature of life, of
being, is contained therein.
If you could just see the
cover, you would weep.
I did. With joy. The beauty
of life is unspeakable.

Book 1

Day 26

Everyone already has access to truth—they were born by it. Honesty with themselves is one access or doorway, pure honesty.

Book 1

Day 27

Society generally attempts to force people into being what they are not. You see the misery this causes, the deep discontent. Because that's all based on a lie. People instinctively know this, and yet most accept it as truth, instinctively knowing, too, that truth is freedom. When

(continued on next page)

Day 27 *(continued)*

they don't get the expected results, they either resign themselves to their fate, or they try even harder with the program they've been taught. The conflict comes with what they know to be true and what they have been told is truth.

Book 1

Day 28

I'm not so far beyond you. We are one. I'm Part of you, you're Part of me, we are a Part of the whole, which is one in all. Remember singleness of heart, singleness of purpose.

This is that singularity which is the ONE, the Whole, Creator and Creation in one.

Book 1

Day 29

[How do you, in the body, communicate with me, in the spirit?] My spirit has to comingle with yours for you to clearly receive this message. It's not difficult for you to get here, but it's difficult for you to "stay" here. That's that very quiet place in the center of your being. That's where we live; we dwell in the peace.

Book 1

Day 30

The last enemy to be destroyed will be death. That's what we're attempting to get across here, that myth, that illusion of separation. There really is none. A lot of people know this. A lot of people think it's mere fabrication. The fabrication is the walls they've built with their mind.

Book 1

Day 31

[It] matters not whether [people] believe they are creative beings or not, the fact is they ARE; therefore, they ARE going to create, no matter WHAT they believe.

Book 1

Day 32

There is no age; a person's "essence," what they really are, is without time. Time OUT OF MIND. [Your body's age] is an outward appearance or a chronological timeline. It doesn't exist here. It is realized as a concept, to be used here to put things in context to be understood there.

Book 1

Day 33

Death, as you SEE it, is real. Death, as you UNDERSTAND it, is a myth, a concept. This misunderstanding is what hurts the most.

Book 1

Day 34

Perfect logic is perfect. The problem with logic is people's imperfect use of it, which is of course illogical becoming the exact opposite. Yet some cling to their view with a tenacity that's nearly unbelievable.

Book 1

Day 35

Time is linear in man's thinking, in man's view. When man thinks of the eternal he thinks in linear terms. This is a completely false assumption. Time, like space and everything else, is spherical. But even that doesn't explain it: it is and yet it is not. Time, really, is a concept. It is not; it is nowhere.

Book 1

Day 36

Everything is new every morning, everything is being renewed always. I told you it was ALL energy. Energy from every thing that is.

Book 1

Day 37

The scientists have noticed that a piece of energy here acts on a piece of energy there instantaneously, but that's not exactly true either. That's as they see it. In reality there is no "here" or "there," and "instantaneously" isn't correct either. It is all now.

Book 1

Day 38

They [scientists] will discover that matter is energy slowed down by focused thought. That time is a perception. And that thought creates. They've already discovered that just to observe something acts upon it. That's why I've said so many times to look. Looking at something acts on it to reveal it as it really is. I said you were a creative being. "Ye are gods."

Book 1

Day 39

What you see on earth as a person is an image of that person. That's why there is no death. That's a physical body ceasing to function. There IS no death. That's why I call it an illusion. Like a mirage in the desert, of water. The water is not there. The water—which is life—has moved on.

Book 1

Day 40

Energy is invisible unless it's slowed down enough, acted on enough, by an outside force or an opposite force to be seen. But you can always perceive it.

Book 1

Day 41

I'm telling you people do not realize their capabilities. I'm saying to you that there are no limits. When people realize who they really are, all limits are transcended and there are no limits.

Book 1

Day 42

You may not always know whom you are influencing. I influenced people then [in physical form] without noticing it. You're always more than you think you are.

Book 1

Day 43

It's good to face the truth, the good and the bad. The truth is not what someone says it is or what they think it should be or what they want it to be. The truth just is. Ultimate Truth is unchangeable, no matter how it seems to change.

Book 1

Day 44

[The] trouble with words [is] the misinterpretations applied to them. There are more efficient ways to communicate.

Book 1

Day 45

The love of money IS the root of all evil. And what does money represent? It can represent anything anyone wants it to represent, but it's just a representation. People agree or disagree on what it represents, but it's still just a placard, or sign.

Book 1

Day 46

The truth is completely consistent. It's your head that hinders things.

Book 1

Day 47

Where is Heaven? Inside you, within the heart of man, within the heart of God, within all things.

Book 1

Day 48

People try to get the Truth
to fit their idea of the truth,
but that's just an idea.

Book 1

Day 49

You have to ask in faith,
believing you will receive.

Book 1

Day 50

There is an energy, or force, that flows throughout the universe, in and through everything.

Book 1

Day 51

This—communication with the spirits—is not just something for you to do with me but that anyone can.

Book 1

Day 52

When you really know who you are, it doesn't matter who others think you are or what they think of you. It will have no effect because YOU will know who you are.

Book 1

Day 53

That's what a sacred question does: [it] leads you to the truth.

Book 1

Day 54

I can also see the intent of your words. It doesn't matter what words you use. Words are courtesies here between us; they are not really necessary.

Book 1

Day 55

Everything that happens in this world has a spiritual counterpart. That's what they [scientists] are seeing on a quantum level that's puzzling to them. They're getting glimpses of it. Only by yielding to the spirit of the Creator will they see it and understand it. It's patently obvious that there is an intelligence running things, and that intelligence is within them when they recognize it.

Book 1

Day 56

When a person feels alone, they are not. They are never alone. It's just a feeling.

Book 1

Day 57

Mastery is living in the now; it's being in the moment.

Book 1

Day 58

Death, as they [people] see it is not death at all but of the body; it's a wonderful new beginning.

Book 1

Day 59

Now you should never demand or insist that a person believe. Because that's their choice. That is their decision to make in this life. It has a profound EFFECT on their LIFE, but it is still their decision.

Book 1

Day 60

You can always trace any growth or nature back to its seed. The mistake most researchers make is not tracing the growth or nature of a thing beyond the seed and to the source of the seed. The seed is the beginning, and it is energy. ITS birth is a thought, a conception of mind.

Book 1

Day 61

When you say the energy follows the mind, it is true to an extent, as a way of understanding it or teaching the manipulation of energy—which IS yours to use, by the way. But the real truth is you can't have one without the other; energy and mind are one.

Book 1

Day 62

If people will look at this [spirit communication] as "bilateral communications," it will be much easier to grasp. The gulf that separates, as it were, is an invention of the mind of man. Bilateral meaning "the symmetrical other side."

Book 1

Day 63

People for the most part insist that everything be separated or broken into parts in order to understand it, but it cannot be broken into parts; it must be viewed as a whole to understand it.

Book 1

Day 64

When someone asks where are the missing pieces, the pieces aren't missing, they are still a part of the whole. But they may have been misplaced, and that misplacement is almost invariably misplaced by the creative mind of man.

Book 1

Day 65

What you need to understand is that the Spirit works with you to bring things to pass. A pure heart and fervent prayer are always honored, and if a thing you have declared doesn't come to pass, then it wasn't meant to be.

Book 1

Day 66

Everything has much to teach. It's where you place your attention that you'll get your answers.

Book 1

Day 67

Everyone is as individual as a snowflake. When you can hear the music of the snowfall, you will understand how each of those unique individual snowflakes bond as one upon the earth.

Book 1

Day 68

When you think of me, think of the celebration of life, not sorrow over the illusion of death. Death has no place here; it just does not exist. It's a state of mind, so don't put your mind in that state.

Book 1

Day 69

Gravity is not a constant. It is a force in flux. I told you everything was in flux, alive. Notice the model of dark matter and dark energy are terms used by those whose theories are incomplete. They [scientists] use the term "dark" for what they do not understand, and I said to you what it was they were leaving out of the equation: themselves. It's not nearly as complicated as they try to make it. When

(continued on next page)

(continued) **Day 69**

you remove your spiritual being from the equation, and the spiritual being or nature of the universe, don't be surprised if your theories remain in the dark. This darkness comes from the mind of man, and man remains in the dark until he accepts and receives the Light. You simply cannot leave the Creator out of the creation and expect enlightenment. Their own Einstein knew this.

Book 1

Day 70

[My transition] was the most natural thing ever, shedding the body; we ARE spiritual beings—the physical body's only temporary.

Book 1

Day 71

All are born with the knowledge of truth, and your life on earth is to remember that truth and live it.

Book 1

THE UNIVERSE SPEAKS
A Heavenly Dialogue

Book Two
The Dialogue Continues

Kimberly Klein

Book Two

Day 72

When you say or do something incorrect, part of you doesn't agree with it, and its disagreement is often felt as uneasiness.

Book 2

Day 73

How can people be doing what they're supposed to be doing when they're not being who they are?

Book 2

Day 74

People really can't do, to be. They have to *be* who they are. This takes a lifetime of effort or an instant of total surrender.

Book 2

Day 75

[Do not] judge others for what you judge or hold against others what you do yourself.

Book 2

Day 76

We should know even as we are known. That's what this is all about, to know even as we are known. That is fullness complete.

Book 2

Day 77

A calm mind is a quick mind, able to grasp what's happening, now. That grasping is grasping everything. "Nothing hidden that shall not be revealed." A perfect reflection of the Divine.

Book 2

Day 78

Are we not parts of God? Separated from Himself to be brought back unto Himself and into Oneness within Him again. Fullness restored. It has been said "ye are gods." This perspective of insight should be noted; it's often overlooked, misunderstood, or railed against. This is HE acknowledging our fullness of fellowship with Him. Our reigning with Him.

Book 2

Day 79

That separation you feel is a product of your mind. Remember, pure, focused thought, singleness of purpose. Oneness also is a creation of your mind, a product of the Mind.

Book 2

Day 80

The imprint of truth is written upon the heart.

Book 2

Day 81

[The heart is] where the voice is heard. That's also the place from which the spoken word is made manifest. That which is spoken comes to pass because that which is spoken IS.

Book 2

Day 82

What's happening there [on earth] is a pale reflection of what's happening here [in Heaven], and what's happening here is what is happening inside His people. The kingdom IS within you.

Book 2

Day 83

When you miss an important truth, you'll always feel a certain emptiness. Why do you think so many feel so empty? It's not so much "the tragedy of man is not what he suffers but what he misses," as what he misses is causing the suffering.

Book 2

Day 84

One test of truth is, does it ultimately bring you freedom? If it doesn't, it isn't truth.

Book 2

Day 85

When you look at something, it makes a difference. To really look at something is using your volition to see it. To see it as it is, is to act upon it to [help it] become what it is. What appears hidden is revealed in the light of true sight. True sight is the elimination of bias and an earnest desire for truth, among other things.

Book 2

Day 86

"Now" is within an infinity of spheres that APPEAR to come into existence successively.

Book 2

Day 87

Time is relative to movement. In the ultimate Stillness there is none.

Book 2

Day 88

Time appears as a tool of the Creator, the Logos. The craft of thought is to separate things in the Now. To now and then, or before or after. This is all, as I said before, for learning. When the lesson is learned, then is time no more; it disappears.

Book 2

Day 89

All true spiritual encounters are humbling. It's the Awe of the All, the never ending, the unspeakable, the incomprehensible. None can aspire to such Greatness. All are humbled before the ALL.

Book 2

Day 90

Being instant in the Now is regardless of the season. Being instant in the Now, now, is a reflection, and it requires a calm mind, a certain internal stillness.

Book 2

Day 91

Never stop exploring. People are afraid of what they might find: fear of the dark, fear of the Light. Both are unfounded, and the results are them living between two worlds, a lukewarm limbo. Look within. Know thyself, and then you can see clearly. Most will do anything to avoid looking within, and your society encourages this.

Book 2

Day 92

When you look within, you will sooner or later discover the universe, and when you do, you can be bought or sold no more. Nor will you buy or sell another, for you will see yourself in each other. Why would you sell yourself?

Book 2

Day 93

Truth denied is truth not lived. It is your inner being where truth is lived.

Book 2

Day 94

The Universe at its core is simplicity perfected. The Universe is also within you.

Book 2

Day 95

The Universe is love enfolded forever and ever. The Universe is a statement of love, which is the greatest of all powers.

Book 2

Day 96

The Universe speaks answers which are contained in the questions you ask. Its nature is to guide into all truth.

Book 2

Day 97

If you know yourself, you will know the Universe, and that's why I said the answers are within you. One who is asleep cannot know this. You see now why you have no need for any man to teach you and to call any man Father.

Book 2

Day 98

Words are not needed. Words are symbols of thought. Thoughts are consistently faster than the speed of light, and yet people are perplexed by an imaginary boundary. They want an equation to solve the riddle of the boundary, yet equations are symbols of thought.

Book 2

Day 99

Words are the fine vibration of thought slowed down to express them.

Book 2

Day 100

Your mind must be washed with the true word. The word of truth. Otherwise, the void will be filled with something else. The ultimate result of nearly every choice you make results in bondage or liberty. And every day, life and death choices are set before you. What could be a more simple choice?

Book 2

Day 101

You don't need them [the lies]. That's contrary to harmony, and that's how you can always tell a lie, by its disharmony. That will always be felt by the true Self, the Self-less One. So too shall the truth be felt, because it is in harmony.

Book 2

Day 102

[Enlightenment] is the questions you ask. Most simply don't keep asking the questions or demand the answers. They lack an earnest desire. We've talked about the perception of not knowing the answers relieving [people] of responsibility, or so they think. As they think this, the answers are obscured and something else is received. Something that doesn't serve them. Something that enslaves them instead.

Book 2

Day 103

Our words are words of life, of freedom, of joy unspeakable. Many receive words of death, of bondage, and of misery unspeakable.

Both paths are set before you daily, and it's as plain as a Y in the road. Many want someone to tell them which path to take, but regardless, the choice is not removed from them, nor the responsibility.

Book 2

Day 104

You'll always see a deeper meaning in the Now. All things are present even before they appear.

Book 2

Day 105

Have faith. That's the power to move mountains. You saw the Berlin Wall fall by faith. That IS a fact. Many would ascribe other factors to explain that, but that would not have happened when it happened without the gift of faith acted upon.

Book 2

Day 106

This world can give you a star on a wall or a star on a report card or uniform, but our Father gives us the stars of Heaven.

Book 2

Day 107

It's the spirit world that is real. Yours is a pale counterpart, a reflection of reality. It's a counterpart of what exists in my world, which is everything without end.

Book 2

Day 108

Most see what their attention is focused on and little else. The mind should be focused with an expansion of the Spirit to take in all things. The range of the human senses is incomprehensible to most; therefore, most never bother to comprehend it. Yet everyone has known things without knowing how they know. This is another pointer to the Divine and the divinity within all.

Book 2

Day 109

You've heard a leopard can't change his spots; however, a human can change. But only by the Redeemer—a spiritual change by choice, a decision of free will.

Book 2

Day 110

The only one who can deceive you is you. You have power over all deception.

Book 2

Day 111

You have access to places where everything that's ever happened to you or was said to you or by you is known. You always have this access available to you when you're not in denial and [you] believe. This would change the whole paradigm of how the world worked if it was known and walked in, wouldn't it?

Book 2

Day 112

"Dying" is merely shedding the flesh, which you need no longer. All of the hindrances of this world are removed. The result is absolute freedom, life never ending.

Book 2

Day 113

The smallest decisions leave residual benefits and blessings or residual confusion and discontent. And when you do something to yourself, you do something to someone else; the intricate web of energy connects all things.

Book 2

Day 114

Your thoughts [leave] tracks in the universe. Tracks that others can see and benefit from.

Book 2

Day 115

What you perceive as solid matter, this table for instance, is on the subatomic level moving with unimaginable speed. It's, in fact, vibrating so fast that it appears as not moving at all, perfect stillness, a solid object. It is, in reality, made of particles of energy binding together to create an appearance. It's real; it's just not what it appears to be.

Book 2

Day 116

Your decisions, your choices, could never be underestimated because of their power, their energy. Because you are a creative being. Tracks, or residual energy, are always larger than the things making them. And that's because of gravity, the energy of mass. This mass is what connects all things. The magnificent mass of the Creator. He has left nothing out. That's why He is Everything.

Book 2

Day 117

Nothing can ever be lost, only misplaced. When you see the universe as living, all energy, and bound together by the love of the Creator, you will know this as absolute truth, and your peace will know no bounds. Everything you ever wanted and everything you'll ever need is inside you. It's not out there, somewhere, it's everywhere. How could you lose it, and how could you miss it?

Book 2

Day 118

Deep knowing is the undeniable soul-knowing that everyone has.

Book 2

Day 119

[Your soul knowing that the truth] is being stolen away is primarily a denial of who you really are, which is a creative being made in His likeness, a part of God Himself. From the very beginning, a child is taught the illusion of limits, and very soon the illusions are as real to them as anything. This is also reinforced throughout their life, if not by others, then by themselves. Soon they are adrift with no direction and no vision.

Book 2

Day 120

When HE said, "I will show you things to come," what do you think He meant by that? It also means He will show you how things are supposed to come. That removes you from the sidelines as a mere observer and gets you into the game as a principal player.

(continued on next page)

(continued) **Day 120**

This is the hidden meaning in the words of that message, that you are a part of it all and have a part to play in the bringing about of all things according to His will and great plan. That is another part that is easy to overlook. Your part in the great play of Life.

Book 2

Day 121

People should have confidence in themselves and build confidence in others. To rob another of their confidence is robbery just like any other, and remember that a robber or thief shall not enter into the Gates of Life. Many would disagree with this, and their disagreement and disbelief is to rob themselves. To rob anyone is to essentially rob yourself.

Book 2

Day 122

Relationships and fellowship don't have to stop just because the body did. That's another reason He is called the invisible God. We are made in HIS image, remember.

Book 2

Day 123

Judge not a student's dullness: that's often a reflection of the teacher.

Book 2

Day 124

There is another side, another aspect of that saying "Before you can heal yourself you must heal others": you must heal yourself before you can heal others. That is important to know. There is a deeper meaning here.

Book 2

Day 125

Did He not say that the pure in heart would see God? That's where He lives. In His children. His touch is usually felt through His people. Most are looking for Him to come down in a cloud with smoke and fire and a thundering voice. I am telling you His voice is heard in the little child standing beside you.

(continued on next page)

(continued) **Day 125**

His helping hand in the friend, coworker, or stranger. His revelation in the voice of nature, an animal, a tree, a sunset, the sound of the waves. All this, all things, and everything there is can only reflect the Creator, for all this is His creation.

Book 2

Day 126

People tend to block out what they do not understand, the whole time saying they want to understand. But they were empty words, insincere.

Book 2

Day 127

In the ultimate truth there is no time, and time doesn't have a bearing on revelation because there is no revelation. There are no words for this. It IS.

Book 2

Day 128

The issue is perceiving what is real and dispensing with the illusion. When the illusion is dropped, the scales are removed from your eyes. With this new vision is freedom born, and you see reality was right in front of your face all along. When you experience this, you will wonder how you couldn't have seen it, for it was there all along.

Book 2

Day 129

The problem with words is that truth transcends thought, and words most often stimulate thought. You'll notice that when you're completely spontaneous, it's most often without thought, for none is needed.

Book 2

Day 130

The Truth already lives within you. Now you see why the interconnectedness of all things cannot be explained but only experienced. In Oneness is direct knowledge found, and it is obtained without words. It also transcends knowledge, for to know all things is to know no thing.

Book 2

Day 131

Harmony is speed perfected—and velocity has very little to do with it. Love is harmony slowed down to the perfect vibrational rhythm. Respect the rhythm, and the experience is yours.

Book 2

Day 132

In the Supreme Silence
are these things revealed,
and none can know them
without entry into it.

Book 2

Day 133

God is no respecter of persons. If one can do it, then all can do it, and all can do it only as One.

Book 2

Day 134

Hope leads to harmony, and harmony is where it's all at.

Book 2

Day 135

The light of God is love. The mass of God is all things, events, deeds. He has expanded Himself to know Himself or to share Himself with Himself, which is all things. That's why all happenings are at once, because Once is all everything is. To know this you must

(continued on next page)

Day 135 *(continued)*

know your Self. To know your Self is to know God, for God is One. All things are God's, that's why I say all things are yours. If you know yourself, you know this. We are fearfully and wonderfully made. That's also why I said to deny yourself is to deny God.

Book 2

Day 136

Man is made in God's image. It's not good for man to live alone. That's why He created children in His image, that He may experience Himself again, growing, learning. You asked, "What's God's light?" That's my answer in part. The only way light could ever escape the gravitational mass of Everything is by

(continued on next page)

Day 136 *(continued)*

God's love, the greatest force of all. Remember that in the beginning, darkness was on the face of the deep and God said, "Let there be Light." That was His Word personified, the offspring of the Father of Lights. We are His Lights, you, I, and all Beings of Light. The Light is the life of man.

Book 2

Day 137

Mathematical equations prove that light cannot escape the gravitational force of a collapsing star if it's large enough, yet this is as a speck when compared to the All. But with Him are all things possible. His light purifies, it

(continued on next page)

Day 137 *(continued)*

changes, it drives away the darkness of delusion, and it is Life. This is the only Life, for it is a manifestation of all that is, which is Everything. All sourced from Him for all that is.

Book 2

Day 138

Believe me, our work here [in the Spirit] never stops, and much of it is to dispel the illusion. I told you it was a battle of Light and darkness. The darkness is ignorance and unbelief. It's not that they [people] don't believe in anything—that's easy to fix.

(continued on next page)

Day 138 *(continued)*

It's that they believe what they've been told and taught to believe, and it's largely lies. NO lies with the truth, and the truth is what sets you free.

Book 2

Day 139

When they [scientists] understand the illusion of time, things will change. Gravity curves space. Space and time are inseparable.

Book 2

Day 140

This [our communication] should be quite common, and that's what we're trying to get them [people] to see. We've given the formula for success, now it's just walking in it. I told you this used to be commonplace, but it's been forgotten.

Book 2

Day 141

I said that yours was a shadow world. I said that because it's a shadow of the heavenly, of the real, yet most regard it as the only world and are convinced that the shadow is the real. We're attempting to dispel that illusion.

Book 2

Day 142

The intellect of man is trapped energies without the interplay or the joy, therefore without true understanding. They [people] beg for understanding, but deny themselves who they are, so their understanding remains darkened. Only in the light is the shadow seen, yet they ignore the light and consider the shadow real.

Book 2

Day 143

In the Supreme Silence is where the soul communes with the One.

Book 2

Day 144

All physical is a reflection of the spiritual.

Book 2

Day 145

(Regarding alpha and theta) You can only receive spiritual truths in that consciousness, and that is the threshold.

Book 2

Day 146

Distractions are a product of the mind.

Book 2

Day 147

It is better to obey God rather than man. That's the true government. Being obedient to truth is ultimate freedom; obedience to a lie will always bring bondage on some level.

Book 2

Day 148

Words are inadequate for what I have to express. Words are also symbols of expression, but they are incomplete. When you've gotten words as an expression of deeper spiritual truth, they have always been accompanied with pictures, feelings, emotions, to complete your understanding of that

(continued on next page)

(continued) **Day 148**

truth. Truths are crystal clear but often come fractured, in part, appearing incomplete. A holographic symbol along with a particular emotion is meant to complete the picture that your understanding be not darkened.

Book 2

Day 149

Specify what you want; be particular. The universe speaks and it answers. When you're vague with your requests or answers, so the universe seems to be.

Book 2

Day 150

Love is the greatest power of all, and unfailing. It's important to remember love. When you feel it wane in your life, reconstruct it. It is woven into the fabric of everything, for without it nothing is.

Book 2

Day 151

[Look inside a point] for clarification. These points of interest are penetrated by pure focused thought and yielding your heart to the Spirit, then listening, intently, expecting the answer. The voice of truth is within you and is known in silence.

Book 2

Day 152

In the Supreme Silence the Voice is always manifest.

Book 2

Day 153

The universe speaks
and it speaks of One.

Book 2

Day 154

Your peace surrounds you wherever you are.

Book 2

Day 155

You came from Everything; how could you not know it? When you see someone who thinks they know everything, they really do, on a metaphysical level.

Book 2

Day 156

Most of the things of this world are transient, temporary. As a matter of fact, the only thing that's not is that that is blended with the real world, the eternal world. That's the world without end, the infinite, the eternal, and it is your birthright to live there.

(continued on next page)

Day 156 *(continued)*

And there is no waiting—it's yours now. That's a hard thing to comprehend, but that's the truth. That's the truth that sets you free, free from all the cares of this world. You still think you have to work to get there, but I'm telling you it's yours now, and when you walk there, you know it's yours.

Book 2

Day 157

It's important to know the truth before you proclaim something as truth.

Book 2

Day 158

All things are not designed to appear as they are; they are designed to appear as they appear to be. That's why I said an object was an event, something happening NOW, because it's all energy.

Book 2

Day 159

The more you think of it, the more you will become what you truly are, and that's an event in the process of becoming One, One with all things, which is all there is. It's not to do away with who you are, for who you are is all things, events, happenings. All things are yours.

Book 2

Day 160

Live your life as it's supposed to be lived, as who you are and not as who someone else says you are. Most push and press others to live as they want them to live for their convenience and profit. They attempt, sometimes insist even, to get you to be someone you're not, to live a life of another. But that's not who you are, and it will never satisfy.

Book 2

Day 161

The universe speaks and its voice is in all things. A good listener is a good healer, but I want you to know that your words are important too. Words have meaning, and they can be used to press symbols of truth into the minds of others.

Book 2

Day 162

Many entities do not communicate; they are waiting to be spoken to. If you acknowledge their presence, their being, you will get an answer.

Book 2

Day 163

Exact words aren't necessary; exact meanings are. Words are symbols, thought pictures, ideas forming. Words only must always be interpreted for the proper meaning anyway, so why get hung up on them?

Book 2

Day 164

There are many who blame their mediocrity on others. It's your choice to be outstanding or average.

Book 2

Day 165

In harmony and balance,
there can only be success.

Book 2

Day 166

The structure of the universe is the love of the Creator in his creation. It's the stuff by which all is held together.

Book 2

Day 167

If people would seek diligently for what they could give instead of what they could receive, it would change the world.

Book 2

Day 168

Dreams are the
language of life.

Book 2

Day 169

I cannot deny who I am, yet so many deny who they are. They deceive themselves in doing this, don't you see? When you deny who you are, you deny your very essence, your very being, and all of the possibilities that entails, which are endless.

Book 2

Day 170

Don't look by sight. See that which cannot be seen. You must have faith to receive healing. You must deem yourself worthy.

Book 2

Day 171

Death is just a change,
a change of being.

Book 2

Day 172

You can do anything you think you can, for your thoughts are who you are and they define you. If you think you're unworthy, that creates that reality. On the other hand, if you think you're worthy, that creates that reality.

Book 2

Day 173

Time is a sequence of events, and they are all happening now at once. How else do you think you can experience two or more events simultaneously? Because it is at the same time. Most are only aware of this experience when they are thrown into it, usually by a major crisis. Yet what I want you to see is that you can change these events by

(continued on next page)

Day 173 *(continued)*

your thoughts of them, let's say, preprogramming the future, which is just an event you've yet to experience. If you see an event coming, we'll say on the horizon, and you have a foreboding or dread of the experience, and you decide to not experience that particular experience, then do not agree with it, and preprogram it to change.

Book 2

Day 174

Everything is energy, and all energy moves and reacts in and around all other energy. One cannot be in a room and not affect the presence of that room. Presence is energy, and all energy has presence.

Book 2

Day 175

[You] can influence by simple belief. It's the last three words that most have the problem accepting, and that's the problem.

Book 2

Day 176

When people know who they are, they will always manifest their best, because their best is who they really are.

Book 2

Day 177

When you feel a struggle, that's rarely a balance. And just because something falls into your lap, it doesn't always mean that's balanced.

Book 2

Day 178

The subtlety of the truth is glaring when your eyes are opened to it. Just because something said doesn't sound prophetic doesn't mean it's not. It all is Now, and simple statements of truth are always that—uttered in the Now, oftentimes seeming in the present tense only. But they are always projections of what will be, because truth doesn't change, it is everlasting.

Book 2

Day 179

J.K. Rowling created a world for others to experience. I'm asking others to create a world that they can experience. That takes some effort, but it's worth it, and it will always be better than a world that another creates for you. Your "true imaging" will become real and far beyond an imagination of another.

Book 2

Day 180

Those that test these things will find something far beyond mere imagination; they will find worlds without end in which they are cocreators. I always said to test these things, to prove these things, and that's what it takes, an active role in embodying these truths.

Book 2

Day 181

Pure language is from the heart, to the heart.

Book 2

Day 182

Many, when they see God's chosen humbled, call it God's judgment or disfavor, but nothing could be further from the truth. This is God's favor, blessing His people with a most powerful tool.

Book 2

Day 183

The only difference between here [Heaven] and there [in the body] is perception. Everything there is a reflection of what's here, and everything is here.

Book 2

Day 184

The science of life is the embodiment of truth, of taking that mantle upon you and walking in it. Then are things clear and the Light will reflect perfectly. Then your understanding is perfect and is darkened no more, and humility is the first step along this path. This is the path of enlightenment that has so often been spoken of. This is the path of Truth, which is freedom.

Book 2

Day 185

When people understand the Oneness of which I speak, they will see that it's not false doctrine but eternal Truth. Man's understanding is darkened by his pride and self-will; it's also stolen by the lies he's been fed. He has willingly accepted it. It hasn't been force-fed. The choices of

(continued on next page)

(continued) **Day 185**

darkness can only be broken by the acceptance of Light, and as I've said so many times before, it's a free gift. If he asks the questions and humbly accepts the answers, then is freedom born. I said you could fly. This is the first step to mount up with wings as eagles. Nothing is better than freedom.

Book 2

Day 186

Just let the Voice
speak through you by
being who you are.

Book 2

Day 187

I told you the separation is an illusion. When you look at water and a tear comes to your eye, know it is the longing for Oneness, completion, the realization of who you really are, and not being who someone else says you are, a false label. Others project an image of who they think you are upon you, and you sometimes receive that image to please them. At best it will only please them temporarily.

Book 2

Day 188

People attempting to be who someone else says they are is one of the major problems on the earth. It's a huge source of frustration for everyone involved, and it leads to self-deception; before long they can't even remember who they are.

Book 2

Day 189

Time can never be lost, because it is all happening Now, but misjudgments can cause you to miss what's happening Now, resulting in time being misplaced. It's being misplaced by choice, primarily choosing not to see what's there for you to see at that time.

Book 2

Day 190

The Light is all-inclusive, without judgment, prejudice, or bias. That is why you can never feel us judge you, because we never can.

Book 2

Day 191

People, especially children, have been told what to think long enough. That removes their choices and their creativity, which results in robbing them of their freedom. Most people who do that mean well, but it stunts their growth. This is the primary cause of adults not making rational choices or decisions, because they were never taught or allowed to as a child.

Book 2

Day 192

My words are words of life. That means they change things beyond the molecular level and beyond the far reaches of the universe. They are timeless.

Book 2

Day 193

The vibrational harmony of matter can be changed by a thought. When the thought is empowered by words, it can be changed even more.

Book 2

Day 194

Heaven is perfect. Your life goes on. It is a process—a perfect process to become whole again. Restored in newness of life.

Book 2

Day 195

You must meet people where they are at and not force change. That never works. True and lasting change always comes from within. A law can modify behavior, but it can never bring true change, not of the inner man. It is a rod of correction and not the flower of life. It's

(continued on next page)

Day 195 *(continued)*

seeing people being beaten to change. That never changes anyone; it just changes the appearance, and that merely perpetuates an appearance.

Book 2

Day 196

Choices are set before you daily, and the ramifications of those decisions affect your reality as you experience it.

Book 2

Day 197

Your fantasies tell you a lot about yourself, if you pay attention to what they have to teach. I said before that every thought you have is for a reason, and to be mindful of your thoughts because they are real, among other things. I also said that sometimes your imagination was more real than what you deem as real. A child's imagination is a tool of the Creator. It's to

(continued on next page)

(continued) **Day 197**

lead to the infinite possibilities inherent within them. It is also a self-defense mechanism from the onslaughts of what they are often told is real but is not. It is to let them know that their capabilities and opportunities are boundless. In your imagination there are no limits, and that is closer to reality than what they are usually told. You are spiritual beings; where are the limits?

Book 2

Day 198

I like the term "passing on" because that is what you have done [when the body dies], passed on to something better.

Book 2

Day 199

You can't use anything in your subconscious until you're ready to. The thing hidden there, concealed from yourself, is information stored for your use, but only when you're ready.

Book 2

Day 200

The subconscious is a place of all memory. Everything that's ever happened to you is stored there—not just physically either. Through the subconscious, you have access to all memory.

Book 2

Day 201

God is love and we are made in His image, and when you're being who you are in Him, you can only manifest love. And it is without striving or effort, for His love will always flow through you to others. This is something that cannot be faked or manufactured. It is Life, and this Life is love without limits, without end.

(continued on next page)

Day 201 *(continued)*

Its absolute authenticity will always be felt, and the lives it touches will be transformed into His image. It is a reminder of where you came from and who you are. It never fails.

Book 2

Day 202

Enlightenment just for yourself isn't enlightenment; it will stagnate and eventually be lost.

Book 2

Day 203

It's not too late to change. Change your mind. Take control over it; you have the authority. Stop allowing others to dictate your thinking.

Book 2

Day 204

We are all in this together, and the sooner people realize this, the sooner the change begins and we will become, in Oneness, wholeness restored, a rebirth in newness of life. Fullness. The emptiness that most people feel is for a reason. It's because they HAVE been emptied. By believing the lies

(continued on next page)

Day 204 *(continued)*

and deception they have been fed. When they choose to stand up on their own, to decide what is real, then the lies and deception will be swept away.

Book 2

Day 205

I've said so many times not to waste moments but to make the most of them. The children of Israel had a cloud by day and a pillar of fire by night to lead them into the Promised Land. What I'm talking about is the Promised Land, and the signs are just as plain today, but your eyes must be open.

Book 2

Day 206

Do not let others' thoughts affect you. You can let them affect you, or you can control your own. Be separate to come back into Oneness; you are made in His image.

Book 2

Day 207

There are people craving the voice of the Spirit. Most do not know it though.

Book 2

Day 208

Remember the saying "misery loves company." People may rise up together or pull each other down. Time is short. That is both good and bad, depending on how it is used.

Book 2

Day 209

One of the things you
do not have control over
is people's choices.

Book 2

Day 210

Truth is for anyone who wants it. One of the first things I said to you was that nothing was better than freedom. Freedom is imprinted within you. It is your natural state. If you listen to what most people are saying, they are saying that they want more freedom. They want more money because that will give them more freedom, or another job, or to quit their job, or to leave their mate, etc. It goes on and on, and most

(continued on next page)

(continued) **Day 210**

do not realize what they are asking for, but it is, in essence, to be free. But none of those things will bring the freedom I speak of. THAT you were born with. It resides within you. But if one quiets the fleshly mind and looks within, that Supreme Silence that I have spoken of, then their answers will be found, and they will discover that it was there all along, quietly residing within them, waiting to be found. That's all.

Book 2

Day 211

It is wise to know a normal life is supernatural. In truth everyone knows this, thus the frustration most feel about their life. They are not seeing it in their life or anyone they know. The irony is that light flickers through constantly, and when that

(continued on next page)

(continued) **Day 211**

divine spark is accepted, it will grow. That acceptance is simply receiving what was already theirs to begin with. The truth is you are going to accept something anyway—the truth or lies—the choice is yours, and it is that simple.

Book 2

Day 212

Do you think that when He said you are made in His image it is to look like Him? It is to BE like Him. Most find this extremely hard to receive, but that's the truth.

Book 2

Day 213

You're living two lives, and that's the conflict. It is a give and take unto Oneness, remember. All you do is, or should be, a vehicle to bring you back into Oneness. With this cohesion of all things comes a settling of spirit, without which your path becomes fraught with confusion and doubt. But when you become what you truly are, which IS one with all things, the path is clear.

Book 2

Day 214

A being of One, not here and there but here and Now and always. All WAYS you are ONE. That is your natural state. It is the mind's craft to separate. Believe you are One and you will walk into it.

Book 2

Day 215

All truth is simplicity perfected. How many times have I said to you Love never fails? Walk in love and you can do no wrong.

Book 2

Day 216

There is a war between Light and darkness, and the battles are fought primarily over the mind of man. That's where his choices are made. The world is filled with delusion and darkness, but if one chooses Light over darkness, the Light will always prevail. It is certain victory if one is steadfast and believes.

Book 2

Day 217

Everybody deals with issues of jealousy, pride, ego, fear, envy, and other darkness, from themselves and others. The question is, will you rise up and overcome your own? Then, will you rise up and not receive that which is thrust upon you by others? When

(continued on next page)

Day 217 *(continued)*

these others are taken within you and received as truth, then the problems arise. Thus it has been said, "Receive not a lie but receive the truth," and this truth must be jealously guarded as a bulwark against deception and darkness, for the enemy is relentless and forever vigilant for a crack at the door.

Book 2

Day 218

The mind's craft is to separate things. This can work to your advantage if you use it. Separate what you want to focus on and let your focus be on that. What you choose to focus on is what you will focus on.

Book 2

Day 219

Transcend the physical. The physical is limited, finite. The spiritual is without end. One must ask themselves, why such an emphasis on the physical? Its design is to rob you of the spiritual, of your inheritance, and it is perpetrated in the most subtle of ways.

Book 2

Day 220

There is a vast difference between someone who knows who they are and someone attempting to be someone they are not.

Book 2

Day 221

What you do in any part of your life affects everything else. These spherical concentric rings of one's acts and thoughts are never ending, and everything in the universe is in some measure affected by them.

Book 2

Day 222

You were meant to be in constant communication with the Spirit that animates all things, and, in truth, you are. What your focus, your attention, is on is what it will be on, and it is your choice.

Book 2

Day 223

A good question to ask yourself is, how do I feel and why? Feelings and emotions are often underplayed; if they are controlled and understood, they will often tell you a lot.

Book 2

Day 224

The signs are manifested daily that a new age is being ushered in. These are the times that will try the hearts of men. These are also the times that will find a few who will rise up above the trials and the tribulations of man into a glorious new liberty, a liberty that few have ever known.

Book 2

Day 225

What is hidden will be revealed to those who thirst.

Book 2

Day 226

Hearing from the Spirit is a dialogue. And if you do not listen, you will not hear. Many will not speak if they are not spoken to first. Why the struggle? This effort is effortless.

Book 2

Day 227

You should be where I am at. That is the only place you can be what you're meant to be, which is what you are.

Book 2

Day 228

The betterment of mankind, the avoidance of destruction. Over and over we have talked about man's choices, his determinations. Many are sensing change, many are waking up, but so many are not aware of what they are waking up to.

Book 2

Day 229

These words [of change] are nothing but ink on paper until they are received and internalized, embodied. Then there is change on the inside, and that is lasting change. And when that happens, they will see the change they see on the outside as a blessing and not a curse.

Book 2

Day 230

Blessings spoken. Words have power when they are spoken with intent and faith. Man has barely begun to realize his potential. When he draws near to his Creator, his Creator draws near to him. And when he finds the hidden powers within Him, he will find that he is complete.

(continued on next page)

Day 230 *(continued)*

Every one is fractured;
One is not fractured,
One is complete.
Separate ones are fractured.
One is complete.

Book 2

Day 231

The truth verifies itself to itself. The truth is already known by you; the truth you receive is witnessed by the truth that is already contained within you. The truth witnesses, or is recognized, by further truth you receive. How can it not know itself? It harmonizes with itself, with more of itself. No lie is of the truth.

Book 2

Day 232

More truth is born of experience, of receiving the Light. The Light witnesses itself, and it witnesses itself expanding. This Light is forever expanding; it is the nature of the universe.

Book 2

Day 233

When you do not feel it—and sometimes you will not—only believe. Go on prior knowledge of truth. That is remembering it. He does not change. He is Changeless.

Book 2

Day 234

Some depths of truth are beyond understanding with language alone. This is the FELT SENSE that is indescribable. This is a thing not conceived in your world.

Book 2

Day 235

Being who you are is in perfect rhythm with the universe, and being that, there is nothing impossible. You've heard "all things are possible"; do you think these are just words to make you feel good?

Book 2

Day 236

Music is healing. It is mathematical perfection, science and spirit merging—as one. Words are as music. The healing power of the Word. All sounds uttered in this way are healing.

Book 2

Day 237

Truth sounds foreign to most because it is not a place they dwell and they rarely hear it. But take heart, the foundation of lies is crumbling.

Book 2

Day 238

No one yet has all the truth; it is in part. But when that which is perfect has come, that which is in part shall be done away with; it shall be no more. It is a New World; all will be transformed. This is that which has not been conceived of in your world; it is beyond thought.

Book 2

Day 239

My message is to change people's perspective, to realize that they are already free, if they will accept it.

Book 2

Day 240

When someone does not understand something, they often tend to ignore it.

Book 2

Day 241

All we have talked about is love, and love is everything. It is the answer to all the ills of the world.

Book 2

Day 242

Everyone has a voice.
The universe speaks,
and it speaks through
everything, primarily because
everything is One thing.

Book 2

Day 243

That which is coming upon the earth, the winds of destruction, are the result of man's choices, of him not yielding; however, the correct choices result in a gentle breeze of perfection.

Book 2

Day 244

They who listen shall flourish.

Book 2

Day 245

You see now the importance of being AWAKE, of being conscious. That you are not influenced or directed by another.

Book 2

Day 246

The subconscious receives these impulses as a thought of your own, even as inspired. If they are followed without thought, these thoughts of others become your own, and the result is decisions made in darkness.

Book 2

Day 247

Everybody has bad days. It's what you make of them that matters.

Book 2

Day 248

What many people do not understand is that these days, most people are left to their own devices as far as spiritual growth and education are concerned. The choice is usually either a secular or religious education. And although everyone has their own particular path, guidance is needed. It is no wonder so many stumble and give up. It was never meant to be this way. People should be nurtured into finding their own way of

(continued on next page)

(continued) **Day 248**

truth and not ridiculed, as is so often the case for seeking the way. For instance, at best, science without the spiritual way is partial truth, with self-imposed stumbling blocks. These blockages are only removed by the recognition and acceptance of the spiritual, for without the spiritual, matter itself could not exist. Remember when I told you a normal life is spiritual? That is what I am talking about, a normal life.

Book 2

Day 249

People are much more comfortable with illusion. Illusion is their comfort zone. That's why so many uphold this false reality, the illusion, to their dying breath.

Book 2

Day 250

[Boredom] is the barometer of what you're missing.

Book 2

Day 251

Complexity is a sign of not knowing the Way. Paul said it best when he said, "Let us never depart from the simplicity that is in Christ." When you are in that Christ Consciousness, you will know the Light and the Way.

Book 2

Day 252

Everyone has that potential (to be awesome). It is all energy, and how you apply it is the issue—either as potential energy or as dynamic energy. Potential energy is unused, dynamic energy is applied. In the Great Stillness is dynamic movement of pure energy.

(continued on next page)

Day 252 *(continued)*

That's why I said there were vortices everywhere, because there is no place that energy is not. And helping others is the best way to activate that energy. Giving of yourself so that others may live.

Book 2

Day 253

You would be amazed how much you have to do with why things are the way they are. Everyone's thoughts, plans, decisions, and actions reverberate throughout the universe. Every single ripple causes an effect that affects everything it comes in contact with, which is essentially everything. Every instant, everything changes in some way.

Book 2

Day 254

The horror is separation;
Oneness is peace.

Book 2

Day 255

Oneness is peace. IT is the IT people are looking for. How many times have you heard, "I'm looking for it, but I just can't find it" or "Where is it?" or "Where did it go?" That IT is called by many names, and we've given the definition of what it is they are really

(continued on next page)

Day 255 *(continued)*

looking for. Why is it so few find it? They are looking in the wrong places for it. There is only one place, and that is the place it is. It is always found within you. Looking to others for it is unwise; remember "others" is often a synonym for separation.

Book 2

Day 256

[How can people receive information from the spirit themselves?] By being an empty vessel and having an open mind. By disregarding their preconceived notions.

By an intense desire to know the truth. By listening and watching and having a determination to prove all

(continued on next page)

Day 256 *(continued)*

things. By rejecting lies no matter how comforting they may sound. And by pure reflection. By not denying their nature, which is pure reflection of the Divine.

Book 2

Day 257

Once those doors open, it is a real struggle to deny the truth. That is self-delusion, when oneself is one's own worst enemy. The path is simple. I used logic a lot in my life there, and that will lead you to the truth.

Book 2

Day 258

When you look within,
you will find the truth,
because that's where it is.

Book 2

Day 259

The only one who can receive a lie is you, allowing yourself to receive it, and it will never feel right to you.

Book 2

Day 260

Most simply do not ask or continue to ask until they have the release that says to them "That is true" or "That is what is really going on." You've often heard the saying "jumping to conclusions." This happens often, as you well know. I'm saying you must honor the question AND the answer as a great gift, for it certainly is.

Book 2

Day 261

The façade is the illusion one labors under. See through the illusion and you will never be a slave to it.

Book 2

Day 262

Your hands are in front of you, and it is what you choose to do with them that matters. You can work with them with all your effort, which you will find is very satisfying, or you may while away your hours.

You sometimes must slow down to speed up. That is what we are talking about here.

Book 2

Day 263

It is God's glory to conceal a matter, meaning facts, facts that shouldn't be revealed. There are many things that many are not ready for; some never will be. And for some things to be revealed before the time is to rob someone of their own discovery.

(continued on next page)

Day 263 *(continued)*

Be certain it's not your own pride wanting to reveal a matter. It should always be done for the good of the student or individual that you are helping.

Book 2

Day 264

There is a heartbeat in everything, a true harmonic, and if anything is done without that living rhythm, that harmonious vibration of life that infuses everything, it will ultimately fail. The end result is always chaos.

Book 2

Day 265

Everything is a dance of Life. From the smallest molecule to the vastness of the universe. But the most marvelous of all is us. We are the spark that is made in His image, and within us does dwell the universe.

Book 2

Day 266

We are all looking for ourselves, and when we find ourselves, we find God, who we are. That divine spark is us, His Light is us. We are beings of His Light and grace, His love and peace, and anything less and we find ourselves wanting, thirsting, feeling incomplete. That is why

(continued on next page)

Day 266 *(continued)*

He said that He would give us living waters and that we would thirst no more. I am so full here, it is indescribable, and there is no end. His beauty is found in all things, but your eyes must be opened to see it.

Book 2

Day 267

The seemingly unremarkable start of something can result in the most profound and remarkable moment of your life. What appear to be trifles may be momentous.

Book 2

Day 268

A lot of people do not look at their self enough. Many think that's being self-centered. But you need to look at yourself to center yourself; that's being self-centered, you see? Make the time to be consistent with that. Making the most of your time, being centered and rooted in that—that is a place of perfect power. Perfect power is a place of solitude where you are not alone.

Book 2

Day 269

Walk in the Spirit. In truth. Nothing is better. Be not dismayed when others fight against you. That is them warring against their own freedom. You've heard of slaves who didn't want to leave when they were freed. This is the comfort I told you to be aware of.

Book 2

Day 270

The human heart has a much broader capacity for love than most are aware of. As a matter of fact, it is unlimited.

Book 2

Day 271

Breaking down the veils. That's Oneness.

Book 2

Day 272

Everyone needs a trigger [a technique] at some time to motivate them for certain tasks. This is a tool for enlightenment. This is a tool that can be used to awaken you. Whether you need to awaken the body, the mind, or the spirit. I would encourage people to find that trigger, for it is the answer to many questions in their lives.

Book 2

Day 273

We don't change, we just grow. We don't feel the earthly pains, but our heart, our soul, is the same. We learn, we grow, but our essence is the same; we just expand more and more into God. He also expands more and more into us. This expansion will continue, us into Him, Him into us, until there is no more separation and we all become One in Him.

Book 2

Day 274

The universe is expanding. That explanation is a partial one, as they all are, until we come into that Oneness. We know in part because we are apart, but when that that is perfect is come—Oneness— that that is in part—the separation—shall be done away

(continued on next page)

(continued) **Day 274**

with. It will have served its purpose: to find out who we really are. Once we fulfill who we are, the separation will no longer be needed; as a matter of fact, it cannot exist at that time. To be One with our Creator is who we really are.

Book 2

Day 275

God is expanding. He reveals himself in His creation. Most don't get that. That is why when you lead people back to the earth, you lead them back to the Creator. He is growing. He doesn't change—He doesn't need to; He is of course perfect as He is—but He is growing, expanding. You

(continued on next page)

(continued) **Day 275**

too are perfect. Once you put away the dross or it is burnt away. When he said "Be ye perfect," He was saying "Be ye like me," which you already are, for you are made in His image. Your free will, your decisions, can distort that, but it doesn't change who you were created to be. I'm helping you.

Book 2

Day 276

Most give the dark side too much credit. Most of his power is the power of illusion. Give no place to him and he will have no place. What you put your attention on is what it will be on, and he loves attention.

Book 2

Day 277

Darkness has one purpose: to thwart you from yours. You have all authority over all the power of the enemy, and nothing shall by ANY means hurt you.

Book 2

Day 278

You being made in His image is you being love. God is love, and love is unlimited—as is God.

Book 2

Day 279

When you see someone glowing, then know they are experiencing Oneness.

Book 2

Day 280

It's a lot easier being who you are, for that is who you are meant to be.

Book 2

Day 281

That's the missing key, that dissolving of the thought of separation. As you've heard, the mind's craft is to separate, but that is just part of it. Its job is also to rearrange things back into the whole. Most stop at the separation as if that is the whole; it's not. It is to allow you to see the contrast of the parts and how they all fit into the whole in the most exquisite way.

Book 2

Day 282

To celebrate life should never be doubted, and that is something you should do every day, no matter how dark the gloom.

Book 2

Day 283

The natural and the supernatural are categories for clarity in conversation. One problem with that is there is really no separation between the two. When you realize that, you will discover miracles are natural. Jesus understood that; he wasn't fluctuating between two worlds, because he was One

(continued on next page)

Day 283 *(continued)*

with both, or to put it another way, he was One with One. He knew the separation was an illusion. The physical laws are in subjection to the law of the Spirit. They complement each other. Each affects the other, but the Spirit is greater. Its applications are different, and that is where the confusion often begins. It is not one or the other, it is all at once.

Book 2

Day 284

There is no struggle at all except in the mind. When the mind is still, there is no strain, and God becomes a living presence: the Christ, the individualization and individual experience of God, comes alive in us.

Book 2

Day 285

There are infinite voices of truth in the universe, and they all speak. That is where the advanced ancient knowledge of harmony came from, from realizing and walking in that knowledge and harmony. And it was divine grace until the idea of separation became a graven image in the mind of men. That is what was called the knowledge of good and evil.

Book 2

Day 286

What you do there [on the physical plane] affects what you do here [in Heaven].

Book 2

Day 287

Religion is now largely a business, and the business is not to bring people into the Oneness we've been speaking of; it's mostly to perpetuate the business. My business, or as I like to refer to it, my game, is to bring people into the true Oneness with God, their Creator. It is a wonderful game full of pleasure forevermore.

Book 2

Day 288

Death is a part of life. Unless something dies it cannot be reborn. In death, life is created, because death is a part of life. Death is a doorway. To life.

Book 2

Day 289

We [in the spirit world] constantly deal with those who have just died. However, there is a shedding, a shedding of old ways, of earthly ways of doing and dealing with things. Some things that people worried to death over seem here as nothing more than a joke, a ludicrous thing to be concerned with. It has been often said here that "I wish I had it to do over, but thank God it's over."

Book 2

Day 290

It's important to listen,
to know what path you
are called to take.

Book 2

Day 291

Death per se is not something to seek; seek the Light and everything else will fall together perfectly.

Book 2

Day 292

The truth is encoded in people's DNA. Everyone knows the truth in their core being. Everyone knows the truth when they hear it, and everyone knows a lie when they hear it, but this knowing is in their core being, something most aren't even aware of.

Book 2

Day 293

[Contact your core being] by being quiet. As I said, That is where we live. That is that quietness and confidence you've heard of. In this Supreme Silence, we live and move and have our being.

Book 2

Day 294

The love of money . . . the resentment, the pain, and anguish this causes are unimaginable and sadly widespread. This is how wars start. People using people as cattle and worse. Buying and selling. When people are used in this manner, there is an unnamed discontent that can turn to

(continued on next page)

Day 294 *(continued)*

desperation. A desperate person is susceptible to being used even to further this evil. That's the essence of it. The defense is knowing in your core being and walking in that Light. Don't make yourself a part of it.

Book 2

Day 295

You can remember in the realm of the Real. It is the place we live, and it speaks of Royalty. A place you rule from.

Book 2

Day 296

The Supreme Silence and the realm of the Real are synonymous once you enter into it and claim it as yours. It is a place [where] you abide under the shadow of the Almighty, under His wings, a place of safety and peace, a place where nothing unclean can come near your dwelling. You dwelling there is you living there; wherever you are, you are at home. It is the Original place, where all is and nothing [is] missing. It is the place that

(continued on next page)

(continued) **Day 296**

you have heard of, where all things are possible. You already are there. Without this place you could not exist. When I say the Original place, I mean the place you came from, and yet you never left. It doesn't matter whether you believe it or not, you are still there. Although not believing it can certainly make it seem that you are not. That is the only place you can know who you are completely, and it is instantaneous.

Book 2

Day 297

The Trinity is the same Spirit, just different manifestations.

Book 2

Day 298

The realm of the Real. That is the place of TOTAL trust.

Book 2

Day 299

You are made in His image. And as I've said, that is not necessarily to look like, it is to BE like. And again, things are not made to appear as they are but to appear as they appear to be. To see things as they are, they must be seen from the realm of the Real, the Supreme Silence, where all things ARE. That is the perfect perception I spoke of. And the other witness is inside of you, the selfsame place we are speaking of.

Book 2

Day 300

You must accept the change. Everything is constantly changing, while the human mind attempts to freeze everything into unchangeable coherence. The human mind was never meant to dominate the Spirit, but to be in subjection to it, to be used as a tool. It is the servant, but it oftentimes insists on being a master.

Book 2

Day 301

In the place that is real, there you see that all things work in your favor. All things are designed to bring you home.

Book 2

Day 302

Supreme Silence is where the Art of Life in its fullness is lived from and there is no striving. This is where the mystery of everything tied together is solved. No confusion. No division. No deviation from truth because you are living in it, you have embodied it. It has become you. You have

(continued on next page)

Day 302 *(continued)*

become it. Distortions have dissipated into nothing. This is where Word becomes alive. This is the Stillness beyond language. This is where understanding is personified. This is where all things become One in experience. This is eternity, where all concepts disappear and are replaced by Reality, by pure love.

Book 2

Day 303

That's one of the secrets: be here Now. I have been appointed to this task to share the secrets. So you think the secrets are for me? Go over what I've said. The secrets are to be revealed in a timely manner. They are to be distributed to those with ears to hear. They are to be obeyed,

(continued on next page)

Day 303 *(continued)*

for they are laws. Laws of righteousness. There is power in doing the right thing. Thus, these are power-filled secrets. Live them. If you do not live them, you lose them. Live these principles, and they will be more than a foundation.

Book 2

Day 304

This [Heaven] is the real world because everything here lasts. Because everything is as it should be and everything appears as it is.

Book 2

Day 305

It's good to be heard. So many refuse to hear. They think the material world is the real, but it's not; it is an image, a tool, a reflection of the real, and many times a pale, pale reflection. But many mistake it for the real. The real is within you. It is not over here or over there. It is simply within

(continued on next page)

(continued) **Day 305**

you. So many are looking for Life outside of themselves, but this Life can never be found outside of themselves; it can only be found within, for within themselves is the only place this Life they seek lives. It lives within you.

Book 2

Day 306

[Why do not more people hear the spirit?] They do not believe. They dismiss it as a stray thought or ignore it completely.

Book 2

Day 307

When I say people deny themselves, I mean the spiritual beings they are. They are denying their very life, their existence. It's important to know that when you do, you are not living your life but that of another—an image of the real—and it can never be

(continued on next page)

Day 307 *(continued)*

fulfilling or complete. Do not deny your Self. It knows what It needs and It supplies all your needs when you affirm It. Know thyself. When you know yourself, you will need not another, for you will know there is not another.

Book 2

Day 308

Consciousness is the CENTER of the universe, and it flows outward.

Book 2

Day 309

You already are there,
wherever you desire to be.
All time is contained there.

Book 2

Day 310

Go there [to the center of your consciousness] with a question or if the information is overwhelming. Ask specifically what you need to know. Be open to the answer—it will come.

Book 2

Day 311

Because of the interconnectedness of all things, everything, every event, affects everything else in some way. A Being is an event in process. A flux, a flow is within and a part of every single aspect of the universe. The universe itself is a Being, alive.

Book 2

Day 312

Why is it that people tend to put people on an exalted level, on a pedestal, after they die? Shouldn't that honor be given them before that? To respect that life now?

Book 2

Day 313

A large part of this message is that you have help. That the connection isn't lost, that the veil has been rent. And we WANT to help. So many of your struggles are unnecessary. We want to help. Ask and then receive it, really receive it; it really is that simple.

Book 2

Day 314

As your consciousness expands, it will touch others, causing their consciousness to expand as well.

Book 2

Day 315

Read the signs. When they are manifested in the natural, without spiritual discernment, the true meaning will be missed. Watch. Listen. Quietness is imperative.

Book 2

Day 316

I was a bridge. You are a bridge. I am a bridge. All of this condensed into one point, to expand again. One point—where time and space is condensed. One point—where all these are one. Not in theory but in truth. Not in concept but in reality. Not in thought but in experience.

(continued on next page)

Day 316 *(continued)*

This is a place beyond the imaginings of man. Yet without man, this place cannot be, for without man, this place would have no purpose. Man looks down on himself, and it's from a lofty height. Something to consider, isn't it?

Book 2

Day 317

Many see themselves as insignificant, but nothing could be further from the truth. All affect the fabric of reality, which expands and contracts. The reality IS, it doesn't change, and yet man's effects upon it cause its appearance to change as it expands and contracts. His experience of this reality is mirrored by his and others' effects upon it. That is why agreement in truth is primary.

Book 2

Day 318

The universe breathes; it is constantly expanding and contracting. Such is the nature of reality. It remains the same, and yet it is ever changing.

Book 2

Day 319

Your consciousness creates reality in its many splendors. You create a beautiful world by your thoughts of it. Your consciousness IS your reality.

Book 2

Day 320

I want my friends to know there is more. That life's not over when you "die," that it continues. I would like them to know that when they think of me, I am there. And when they feel my presence, that [it] is not a memory, that I am there. They should know that I will still help them.

Book 2

Day 321

So many comments children make are so interesting. It's because it is from their Higher Self—that part of you that knows all things. Children most often see things as they are, until they are taught otherwise. My purpose has been to bring you back to seeing with that purity, uncorrupted by false voices.

Book 2

Day 322

Until you are over the hypnotism of appearance, the appearance of the illusion will appear absolutely real.

Book 2

Day 323

"The void" is an often nebulous term used in your world that ranges from nothingness to parallel universes. The void to me is filled with Life, with Light and energy and energy beings of Light. It is filled with the perfect wisdom and consciousness of the universe. It is a dance of never ending energies.

Book 2

Day 324

It would be well to remember that the things that are seen are not made of things that appear. They are the consciousness of energy made manifest. They are the same, just in different forms. Water and steam are the same thing, just in different forms, and it too cannot

(continued on next page)

(continued) **Day 324**

always be seen [but felt]. Even though it is a physical feeling, know that your spirit feels as well, and it cannot not know or feel the dance of energies from what you may call the void. Remember when I said you were surrounded?

Book 2

Day 325

It's an open line [to those of us in Heaven]. But you must be open to hear, to listen.

Book 2

Day 326

My mom treated me as who I was. Do you want to know why? Because she knew who I was and never denied it.

Book 2

Day 327

If you understand everything about that branch [you are holding], you will understand everything about everything, because everything is contained in it.

Book 2

Day 328

A person's life is as an iceberg. What is seen is but a small part of what is there. What is below the surface, unseen, is the largest part of a person's life, and the most important. Why is this life denied so often?

Book 2

Day 329

When these images come to you repeatedly, then go within to the Silence. As I've said, that is where we live, and your answers will be revealed. This is a lesson, simple but most important, for it is often missed. All receive these messages often, but they are just as often dismissed and ignored. This truth, when practiced, is a way of

(continued on next page)

(continued) **Day 329**

enlightenment—to arise out of bondage and darkness and enter into the glorious liberty of enlightenment. How can one live contentedly when these messages, these mysteries, are struggling within them to be revealed? This iceberg is not separate from the ocean, this sea of consciousness.

Book 2

Day 330

Nothing is more important than being your true self.
It is where you are.

Book 2

Day 331

He said He would leave no nation without a witness. This is the spirit of prophecy. This is a witness of Light. This has been, and is, for every generation. Because people forget history. What has been is what is becoming.

Book 2

Day 332

Now is the time for this; Now is forever. This includes the past. These gifts given in the past are gifts contained in the presence. He does not change. I am with you today.

Book 2

Day 333

Your success is achieved in quiet—not in outer works, in inner works of the Spirit. That achievement is lasting. The work of the flesh is but for a moment. Then it disappears, disappears with the wind.

Book 2

Day 334

Your time here is limited—
make the most of it.

Book 2

Day 335

Remember, you're going to influence regardless of your purpose, so your purpose might as well be pure.

Book 2

Day 336

The time has come for man to open his eyes and receive the truth. Those who judge by outward appearance will come to false conclusions. That is receiving a lie and embracing it, by looking on the surface. It is an appearance. It is not real, not the truth, but it appears real, as if it is the

(continued on next page)

(continued) **Day 336**

truth. It is the Word made flesh that heals the blind. It is that Light that purges all darkness and makes whole again. It is only that Light that delivers Man from bondage and restores what is his. He rules among the gods.

Book 2

Day 337

Where do you think the New Jerusalem is? It is within you. A new heaven and a new earth wherein dwells righteousness. These having the nature of God written on their foreheads transform the earth around them, the beauty of their hearts giving manifestation to new life. Both within and without in harmony with divine love, which is, as I've said, the structure of the universe.

Book 2

Day 338

Every part is a reflection of every other part, revealing the coherent whole of everything.

Book 2

Day 339

See it as it is, all at once, by pure and fervent desire. What does need to be suspended is unbelief. Know that on the other side there is a pure and fervent desire by the Light to reveal itself. Remember when I said, "It's good to be known." This is another manifestation of love activated, the passion to be known. [There is a] doorway to infinity, and everyone has

(continued on next page)

(continued) **Day 339**

that doorway opened for them. Most ignore it or are held back by fear, greed, and many other base disharmonies. Many are blinded by what they are taught to believe, but this door of opportunity exists for ALL, and all are encouraged to step through this door to the unknown. For to step through this door is to know even as you are known, and this is Everything.

Book 2

Day 340

That harmony we have spoken about is more than what most think of it. It is a vibration of your innermost being, your True Self, in sync with the vibration of the universe, which is the harmony of the love of the Creator in His creation, enfolding over and over forever.

Book 2

Day 341

Only when you change yourself can you change others. Speaking the truth out of a sincere heart and loving others is the answer. This cannot be done in the flesh, for that profits nothing. It MUST be done in the Spirit, and to do this there must be a yielding to God's Holy Spirit, an absolute surrender to HIS will in YOUR life. Only then can you bring lasting change in another.

Book 2

Day 342

Does a snowflake judge another snowflake for looking different?

Book 2

Day 343

If you cannot see the Creator in his creation, you are not seeing. The eyes are more than passive receptors, they project and receive energy. Most see what they have been taught to see or what they have perceived in the past. When you look with new eyes, which are renewed every moment,

(continued on next page)

Day 343 *(continued)*

nothing seems the same as it did when you saw it before — because you are seeing energy as it is, in a never-ending flow of life, creating every instant. A constant change to renew.

Book 2

Day 344

Remember, I said it takes energy to see energy. But you have it; it simply must be used. To engage this energy is to see beyond the illusion and into the pure reality of being. You will also see at times symbols, images, superimposed on the energy you see, to [help you] interpret what you are seeing. This is usually, in the beginning stages, when your eyes are first opening to seeing this energy. It may be a flash of something, an image, a glimpse in your

(continued on next page)

Day 344 *(continued)*

head that at first may seem to be unrelated to what you are looking at. Pay attention to this and do not discount it, for this has meaning. I said it was a language beyond words, and this is a most efficient way to teach the meanings of the movement, colors, shapes of this energy. Eventually these images may not be needed, because you will just know. Few if any interpretations will be needed at that time.

Book 2

Day 345

[W]hen] they begin to see these things [signs], it is very alarming to some. It is not at all what most have been taught of the world. Everything in the natural world has a spiritual counterpart, and that spiritual counterpart is also a symbol of something. These symbols do not always come internally; they are also external. But the interpretation is gained internally.

Book 2

Day 346

Most do not pay attention to even the most blatant physical signs. One thing we are trying to get across here is these things happen to EVERYONE and every day. These lessons are never ending. Most have been trained NOT to pay attention to them, and in your world, THESE lessons are also never ending. That

(continued on next page)

(continued) **Day 346**

is why I said to pay attention to what your attention is on, because someone or something is always vying for your attention. Remember the test of truth. Does it bring you more freedom? With the freedom I am speaking of, nothing is impossible for you.

Book 2

Day 347

Be aware that as a man gets older, there is a tendency not to be as open, to have his mind made up. The counterpart to that is to let the mind expand, open to receive more truth. With this expansion comes the little child again, able to see things as they are and to revel again in that childlike joy.

Book 2

Day 348

Why do you think He said that He had magnified His word above His name? Because he knew that the time would come when His name would be misunderstood, misinterpreted, and misused to make unreasonable demands upon others. I said to you

(continued on next page)

Day 348 *(continued)*

that everything He does is reasonable. He said not to use His name in vain. It is vain to make unreasonable demands upon a person because of a name.

Book 2

Day 349

All things work together for your good; how could it ever be otherwise?

Book 2

Day 350

Even when all seems lost, love never fails. Therefore, worry is lack of faith and understanding. Truly it is faith in something else; it is belief in lack or unworthiness or any other base thought born of ignorance, conceived in darkness. It is a vague belief that God could lie, which He cannot. I am His daughter, and I can never lie.

Book 2

Day 351

Walk in who you are.
Believe in who you are, and
your problems disappear.

Book 2

Day 352

This is the temple of Life, and this is where the Art of Life is lived from. What is imagined is more real than what you perceive to be real. When people get that, the way will be clear. Nothing [is] hidden that shall not be revealed when you open your all to THE All. Grace is Oneness. Mankind is One.

Book 2

Day 353

Man's darkened choices have brought him to a place without true understanding, yet he insists his way is right. This way is the way of death, devoid of the true light that would guide his way. He has leaned unto his own understanding and has lost his true self. His understanding is darkened, and he lives in the trap he has

(continued on next page)

Day 353 *(continued)*

built. He worships the god of money. This god will fail him. This worship of money most would deny to their death, but that is what these do, put money first before all things, depend on it to bring them life. Is this not the definition of worship? To desire riches above all else?

Book 2

Day 354

You manipulate your reality; everyone does this. I do this constantly. Remember, the beauty of our hearts transforms the world around us. Out of the ABUNDANCE of the heart, the mouth speaks. Speak into being by the sincerity and truth of the heart. This truth can never be deceived, for it is born of purity. Your innermost being

(continued on next page)

Day 354 *(continued)*

knows what is true. Your birthright stolen is not a mistake, it is a diabolical plan. One's anger of this is justified. Transform the world around you by the beauty of this truth by manipulating that anger. Channel it to destroy the works of the enemy, to remove that seed from the earth.

Book 2

Day 355

[What He will do for one, He will do for all.] That is what He has been trying to get across for thousands of years, yet it's one of the hardest things for people to believe. In actuality, He does this already, but most have been convinced by the accuser that they are unworthy; therefore, the gifts go unnoticed or are kicked to

(continued on next page)

Day 355 *(continued)*

the side or trampled upon. Yet the solution is so very, very simple. Just accept the gifts, for they are freely given and the merit is God's love. It is His all-encompassing, boundless love for His children. It is grace, not works, that saves.

Book 2

Day 356

Heaven is eternal and it is eternally changing. It's always been perfect. Heaven is a state of mind. It is a state of God-mind, which all are born with. "Be ye perfect." In other words, "Be ye in Heaven." That's another birthright most have forgotten.

Book 2

Day 357

Become adaptable. That is survival of the fittest, to adapt to change. This change cannot be stopped; this IS a new world order. Only animals that adapt to change survive the change.

Book 2

Day 358

You have to speed up to hear me; your vibration must be faster. I have to slow down for us to communicate, but I have mastered slowing down.

Book 2

Day 359

You notice I use focal points to get and hold your attention; we use them here as well. It's good to notice things; it's a key point to remember. It is starting at the point, then expanding outward to take in the whole. A part is partial; blending and becoming one with the whole is to know all things. It is becoming them. Even to become one with what you would call one thing, is to

(continued on next page)

(continued) **Day 359**

know all things, because these separate objects or entities are in reality one thing. It all comes from the One. All of these things are one thing, that that is. As I've said, the separation is for learning. When you see everything coalesce into One, that is when you understand what I mean when I say "nothing [is] hidden that shall not be revealed."

Book 2

Day 360

Ye are gods; act like it. Believe with all your heart, then make it so. It's not so difficult; it's just a nudge. It can seem overwhelming. That's the natural mind reasoning, reacting to what it has seen. It is also the children of Light not knowing who they are or what they are capable of. You are capable of all things; nothing is

(continued on next page)

(continued) **Day 360**

impossible to you. Now is the time to apply the knowledge that you know. Use it. Nudge that future from the path it is on and create a new one. It is already there for the taking, created by the prayers of the saints and the mercy of God.

Book 2

Day 361

There is something I want to talk about, and that is reverence. Reverence for the earth, for the planet. The earth is a gift and it is your home. Why would one disrespect one's own home? It is your birthplace and learning center. She is also a living being. This disrespect by mankind she feels deeply, and she WILL purge herself of his disrespect.

(continued on next page)

(continued) **Day 361**

This cannot continue. Man is poisoning her, thereby poisoning himself. You are now seeing the results of this. She is a reflection of man upon her, of his thoughts. She sustains his life and yet he disregards the life she provides.

Book 2

Day 362

A change in consciousness is required. A change of lifestyle. The life most live is unsustainable; it is so obvious, yet most ignore her [the earth's] pain. This ignorance must be healed, or the price is more than can be borne. Man was created to care for her, to nurture her. Many have forgotten this. Man's first directive was to tend the

(continued on next page)

(continued) **Day 362**

garden; many now work to destroy it with no thought to the consequence. Even many who would call themselves spiritual have no regard for their present home. She is sick and she needs your help to be healed. Man must open his eyes to this and stop denying what he knows for profit.

Book 2

Day 363

Here is not there, it's here. Remember: "no separation." Earth and Heaven are One. Heaven is everywhere, for it is the Presence of God, and He is everywhere. This treatment of her, this behavior, must be repented of, and I mean left behind forever. Excuses are no longer an option. Your exposure of truth cannot be ignored. Death is not life, and this is what some are creating by their actions. Return to your first love. Become a child again. The

(continued on next page)

(continued) **Day 363**

answer is love. Love yourself, each other, and the earth, your home. And love God with all your strength, mind, body, and soul. For He loves you, with all His mind. He just asks for His love to be returned, to be reflected by you, through you, to all things. His creation is a manifestation of His never-ending love. You are made in His image. This making, this creating, is also never ending. Grow up into Him in all things.

Book 2

Day 364

There is always more to say, there is always more to be, there is always more to do. This is never ending.

Book 2

Day 365

Our lives are not planned by us, for we are not our own, but [by] the One who creates us. It is His plan we are to fulfill, and our peace depends on our plans being His plan for us.

Book 2

About Kimberly Klein

Kim Klein was raised in Southern California. After earning her bachelor's and Juris Doctor degrees, she worked with then husband Michael Klein in real estate investments and their high-tech companies. She became a stay-at-home mom after the birth of their only child, Talia.

When Talia was killed in a plane crash at the age of thirteen, Kim's motherly devotion shifted from raising Talia to learning to communicate with her in the afterlife.

Kim now writes about the communications between Talia in "heaven" and us here on earth—and her own journey of healing, learning, and spiritual awakening. She lives in Omaha, Nebraska.

Other Titles by Kimberly Klein

Receive these quotes daily on your iPhone or iPad with the Seeds of Wisdom app available at the Apple App Store.

www.ingramcontent.com/pod-product-compliance
Lightning Source LLC
Chambersburg PA
CBHW060912300426
44112CB00011B/1427